C

GW01466536

Also by Tom Pickard:

Poetry

High on the Walls, Fulcrum Press, London
The Order of Chance, Fulcrum Press, London
Dancing under Fire, Middle Earth Books, Philadelphia
Hero Dust, New and Selected Poems, Allison & Busby, London
Domestic Art, Slug Press, Vancouver
In Search of Ingenuous, Slug Press, Vancouver
ok tree, Pig Press, Durham

Fiction

Guttersnipe, City Lights, San Francisco

History

Jarrow March, (with Joanna Voit) Allison & Busby, London

CUSTOM & EXILE

Tom Pickard

ALLISON & BUSBY
LONDON & NEW YORK

First published 1985 by
Allison & Busby Limited
6a Noel Street,
London W1V 3RB
and distributed in the USA 1986 by
Schocken Books Inc.
62 Cooper Square,
New York, NY 10003.

Copyright © Tom Pickard, 1985

British Library Cataloguing in Publication Data
Pickard, Tom
    Custom & exile
    I. Title
    821'.914 PR6066.I25
ISBN 0–85031–657–X–Pbk
ISBN 0–85031–667–7 Limited Signed Edition

Set in 11/12½ Bembo by
Falcon Graphic Art, Wallington, Surrey
Printed & Bound in Great Britain by
Biddles Ltd, Guildford, Surrey

Contents

Acknowledgements

All of these poems were written between 1979 and 1985 except for "Coil Mistress" which was written in 1972.

I would like to thank the editors of Pig Press which first published some of these poems in a pamphlet entitled *OK Tree*: also Slug Press in Vancouver which published *Domestic Art*, and *In Search of Ingenuous* as signed limited broadsides. Thanks, too, to Bill Swainson, my editor at Allison & Busby. Thanks are also due to Neil Astley.

Thanks to the editors of : [in the **UK**] *Ninth Decade*, *New Socialist*, *Tribune*, *New Departures*, *Here Now*, *Poetry & Prose* (Warwick University), *Poetry London*, *Apple Magazine*: [in the **USA**] *The World*, *Friction*, *Ink*, *North Dakota Quarterly*, *Poetry Project Newsletter*, *Hawaii Review*: [in **Australia**] *Scripsi*.

Most of these poems were first published in public performance and I would like to thank the organizers of those events in **Germany:** Dept. English at Seigen University; Workshop l' Poésie Europe, Frankfurt; British Council (Koln, and Hamburg); Buch Handlung Welt, Hamburg. **Holland:** Literaire Instuif, Haarlem; One World Poetry, Amsterdam; Paradiso, Amsterdam; Melk Weg, Amsterdam; Literary Café, Den Bosch; Poetry International, Rotterdam. **Yugoslavia:** Writers Union, Belgrade, and Novi Pasza. **Belgium:** Beursschouwburg, Brussels. **Canada:** Harbour Front, Toronto. **USA:** The Poetry Project, NYC; Committee for International Poetry, NYC; Bernard Jacobson Gallery, NYC; White Columns Gallery, NYC; SUNY at Buffalo; Albright-Knox Art Gallery, Buffalo; Allen Town Community Centre, Buffalo; Just Buffalo; Jack Kerouac School of Disembodied Poetics, Colorado; University of Colorado at Boulder; Patterson College, New Jersey; Worcester State College, Mass.

For Joanna

our love is a bird in flight
  and each lost day
    and night
  is a feather torn
from its exquisite wing

    for long
and graceful flying
  each part
of its immaculate plumage
    should remain intact

Signed and Dated on the Lover
Ingres: La Grande Odalisque

blue velvet november
    bleached blue
bed and pillows

a peeled off
    burnt-gold dress
still warm in folds
    swells parallel
to her swimming descent

a blush of peaches
    in a bowl
by the bed

her arm
    lies
    along her length
and tapers
    into
an enclosed palm
    which smooths
a bone-handled fan whose
    peacock
    tail-feathers flutter
flicking licks along
  the inside surface
    of her
      thigh

Portrait of a Widow
Abraham Lambertsz van der Temple

The young blonde widow
in the black velvet dress
whose unsprung curls
spring around a string
of rolled spit pearls
holds
a white peony rose
as though it were a fig-leaf
just plucked
from Cupid
who now stands
naked
behind her.

Diana at her Bath
Rubens

Diana,
her nipple
kissed pink
by the red dress
so recently removed
and rolling
the low light along
its narrow folds,
slips
a white silk shift
above her head
and sees
she is
revealed.

Move on
before her followers,
their heads
towards
some sudden happening,
turn
and trap us
in the act
of seeing.

French Kiss

a ponce in Pigalle
    with an Italian blade
in his pants
        has a girl whose
smile slashes slices off
    the moon's face

a mechanical bird
        a negro sells
flies flapping
        in dizzying circles
like a street ballerina
        tap-dancing
a tango
        on cloud

Words

my head held
between your thighs
a warm flower
opening at night
a strange letter
sleep brings
music
a bird
in your bush
sings

Verboten te Meren

When Angie Baby
of Panama,
getting a pull
off Eros
in the Nieuwe Maas
at midnight,

kisses,
her lips stick,
tasting a tongue-cup
of come.

Blue Brood

a high-skyed
      late August afternoon,
      my wife sleeps:
whispering
      (white clouds
blown from the west)
  of trembling leaves,
      silenced
by a passing train
      travelling
nuclear waste
      along
the track
to the coast

cumulus
      swells to
fluffy toys
      thighs
curled to
      touch
her swollen belly
      she listens
to my heart
      beating
her own
      is heard
by a third

I feel like
      a hen
hatching
      an egg

Portrait of a Woman Walking

pregnant
she stopped to look at
a boxer bitch
with dark nipples

not bad,
good shape,
no belly

balancing a blade
on her finger tip
she taught it
         to skip
and stick

chased swollen berries
in pricking brambles

the corner of her mouth
got stained with juice

we licked it off

Goya Sketching

She has a quick sensitive face:
self confident and alert.
I take notes,
like a policeman
loitering in an alley doorway.
We compare notes, and
they compare.

★

Solona, tired

She walks out of the room
but remains in the painting.

Will you come back tomorrow?

*So you can take me
from myself?*

Goya strokes shadows off
her lips.

*Part of us is always lost
to another.*

Sprig

of lilac
   in a glass
of clear water.

Hurry-along-ash,
    always last
to laugh,
    touched green
by the sweeping
      dab
of a sable
    brush.

Two sparrows fuck,
    delirious
in a dust bath.

Stuttering primroses
on a south
    facing bank.

Dusk drifts in,
  a slut
in a loose blouse.

Early evening
    casts
long shadows
   on the grass.

Tern

waves fly from the sea
towards you
a flock of panicked gulls
their wings
brush against your tits

a smooth head parts your lips
black eye reflects an eye
death drops a seed
and sleeps

Owl

almost
perceptible

warm breath
wings in my ear

On a Dutch Beach

Breakers belly and swell.
As she turns her head, afraid
of a moon–lit lighthouse tower,
the swollen tide tugs at her hips.
She grips a wave-thrashed post
to push her patulous cheeks
into the face of a slapping sea.

A glowing string of broken sperm
clings to her flowing hair.

Swimming through a galaxy of phosphorus,
stars drip from her arms and dissolve;
whole new constellations ripple into shape,
and break.

Coil Mistress

come wet belly
        shock of windows
    fingers on a wineglass

thighs entwine
    crumbling walls
stale and still
        any unlit terror
possible

I drew two snakes
        took a woman's shape

    in your hand mine
            in your eye mine
fire flame
            companion
sister sister mother daughter
        snake snake snake

OK Tree

ok tree
you can bloom
Spring's arrived
with two green eyes

In Search of Ingenuous

opening a dictionary
between inflict
and inhuman

my eye falls
on a flower
placed there
and preserved
by you

seeing
informs
my heart
infolds

★

between idolize
and ILO
a violet
whose moth petals
hover on
ignotum per ignotius

explanation
obscures the object

Domestic Art

on a white
cabinet

in our three
blued
bathroom

she has folded
over a glass dish
of abalone shells

a bright pink
facecloth

Whorl

The women
        selling gladioli
on Nowy Swiat
        hold up
thrusting bunches
        of signalling
            colours.

She selects those
        rarely hued
(avoiding blood red, but
        when given them
        as gifts
    quickly regives
to guests,

cutting
        frayed inches
    from the otherwise
            taut stalks
of those remaining)

and plucks, daily,
    into her palm,
with three fingers
    and the heel
        of her thumb

the dead
        and withered
    calyxes.

White Room

the street outside
is quiet with rain

in a white room
I stroke your long back

hold my shoulder
you sigh and yawn

opening your eyes
to another morning

Warsaw Autumn, 1981

that sudden rumbling
of a sheet of tin
trembling

as it's hoisted
over wooden
scaffolding

to the vestry
rooftop

Letter to Joanna,
Warsaw/London Express

half awake from a rough night's ride,
an old Polish peasant's back hurts

he cuts pieces off an apple
which sizzles at the steel assault

his big hands slice slivers of skin
with a knife which is a friend to him

his familiarity with the blade
is ancient

passing me the fruit, he gestures:
to refresh the mouth

on the edge of our seats
we gaze at the land

with the confidence of dawn
he mutters

*

thick mist through dark woods
your scent on my scarf

we roll slowly
over another border

ps: Berlin

outside every unlocked door
        soldiers stand
legs spread
        thumbs tucked
            in gun-belt buckles,
like insolent cowboys

another leads
        an unmuzzled German wolfhound,
pulling on its chain,
        as they search above,
        below,
and through the belly of our train

No News

We've been apart too many seasons.
Between this and the last breath
I have aged a millennium.
TV located in the corner of the livingroom.
Someone is born and named.
We learn to live with the moments
not to despise the days.
The empire establishes another colony
of stateless terrorists.

THREE FOR NYC

Valentine

so,
soft
lips,
amid
sky-
kiss
buildings
be
mine

Off Cast

crouched over
in a Bowery doorway
an old coat's forgotten
no one wears it
anymore

Spring

tall slow Sunday sunset
over the West Side Highway

walking down Hudson
thinking of you

two dogwoods bloom
in a doorway

Shedding her Skirt

I had forgotten
how to be
apart from you
and taught myself
tonight old tricks

should they have
their fusion?

colonize space?

the silence here
is different

a room
surrounded
by rooms

where is our
world?

are we in it?

noises all night
of sentences
I had forgotten

and in the remembering
forgot again

If that Sod left me in Peace

It only lasted two weeks
then I couldn't stand the sight of him.
He married me out of pity:
he knew I didn't love him.
The Social Security made me take out a summons
for desertion. I told them
I didn't want a thing and glad to be rid of him.
They went mad in court.
But it's not his bairn, and I don't want his money.
I just want to be left alone.

The doctor gave me some pills:
but I get agitated
and can't get done,
then I lose me temper
and get ratty with the bairn
and think *I'll kill him*
and there's nobody here to stop me.

I was lucky getting the flat.
I couldn't manage without it.
Mind you we've got rats
from the dere' factories.
I found one on his cot.
They come for the crumbs,
and eat their way through a loaf.
The council put down poison.
I hope he doesn't find it.

He eats like a horse, the little get;
he eats more than I do.
Me sister said she'd take him,
if her man gets a job down in London.
She thinks the world of him, mind,
and he'd be happy with her.
But I don't know.
If that sod left me in peace.

To my Son on his 16th Birthday Declaring himself Gay, December 1980

the sky over Warsaw
  is the grey belly
of a snow bird,
      brooding

pigeons flutter
          past the window
like early flakes

      in a dream
a talking hedge-sparrow
      with a starling's
speckled shimmer
    said *hello*
and *compendium*

we worried
  about finding it
a mate
  neither too wild
      nor dull

winter trees
  by the river,
like tongue-licked
        feathers

May Storm in the Rockies

spray painted
      spring foliage
against utility
           evergreen

spruce pine
     on a cold wet
   mountain

snow,
   thick as a fur coat,
wraps over tree tops—
  embracing a peak

May I Bring you my Head on a Plate?

not just something
to put on the head

caps

can be got under
come into from beneath

not just something
to sip from

caps

can be doffed in deference
to a toff

not just something
to throw in the air

caps

can imprison you

Terminal Circuit

the grey haired
        German poet
with a Lech Walesa
moustache
    who switches his
vodka with
    my water
while falling
  over a table
shouts
CIA!
    and grabs
the French girl
    in red silk
pyjamas
  who takes
    my photo
    with a flash
        as she
  falls

Solidarity

protesting
    outside New York's
  Central Street Court
   a black dissident chants

free Amiri Baraka
   free Amiri Baraka

others
    hold up placards
  saying
   no justice
in America

and

stop racist murders
    in Atlanta

one
  of four children
on the picket line
    gazes towards
a hot dog stand
   who's vendor
    leans close
to hear
   the news

A Knife Shop in Nato

A glistening avalanche of polished surfaces
and sharp icy slopes.

A dagger which spits erect
when a steel button in its neck is pressed.
Knives with classical proportions.
Small secret knives for women as a last resort.
Cavalry officers' swords which salute in their scabbards.
Heavy-handed butcher's knives for paring flesh.
Knives for hire.
Knives for narcophants.
Knives with serrated blades for ripping meat and chipping
bone.
Knives with hooks for howking out gut.
Knives with dangerous tempers.
Knives with a love of wood.
Knives with a desire to kiss trees.
Knives with a taste for blood.
Knives which demand obedience.
Knives to grip in the fist and slash with.
Knives with black handles like Macedonian midnights
studded with dog-bark rivets and fighting-cock cries.

And small hand-held mirrors
for gazing steel into the eye.

Sweet F.A.

There's victory drunk and defeat drunk
Relegation league-drop and promotion drunk
Board-meetings and bent-manager drunk

There's league-table drunk
And cup drunk
And World-Cup drunk
Finalist and semi-finalist drunk
Newspaper-and-television drunk
Hat-trick and soccer-hooligan drunk
Trainer drunk
There's former-star-player-turned-pundit drunk
Poor-attendance drunk
Shaking-hands-with-Prince-Charles drunk
And winking-at-Lady-Di drunk
There's colour drunk and shirt drunk

There's away-game drunk and home-game drunk
Alcohol-forbidden-on-the-terraces drunk
Referee and linesman drunk
Offside drunk
And half-time drunk
There's final-whistle and injury-time drunk
Foul and player-booked drunk
Special-cells and teach-them-a-lesson drunk
Short-sharp-shock drunk
Stiffer-penalties drunk
Bring-back-the-cat drunk
Magistrates and mascots drunk

There's right-winger-MacGregor-dribbling-
in-the-press-box drunk:
*Mr Scargill and his 80% minority have
moved the goalposts* drunk
Thatcher-Fowling-the-pitch drunk
Starve-them-into-submission-and-call-it-a-draw drunk
Pickets-police-battoned-and-booked drunk
Leon-and-his-bovver-boys-in-blue-
sticking-in-the-boot-for-Brittan drunk

Carlo Crivelli's Saints Jerome & Augustine

Saint Jerome's red hat is held
by a long anchoring chord
to his navel.
The temple of God is balanced
in his hands like a toy.
A flash of light:
someone inside is vomiting blood.

Saint Augustine's jewel–encrusted fist
claws a crooked pike.
The papal crown is a galaxy of satellites:
precious stones in orbit
around his head.

A lion gazes up in adoration
of its master: mane well groomed,
teeth and claws bared.

Dissent is interned
in temples.

A Sense of History

along the banks of the Tyne
     to look
        for driftwood

  dawn
    mist over water
the great stone railway bridge
  with blackened arches

a couple—pensioners—
      bent and stiff
scrape the dry earth
    with wire sticks

    they hack hard clarts
collecting
      small bits of coal
    dust almost
      baked
  in frozen mud
           and clay

Mutiny

The Admirals brushed
the dandruff off their
epaulettes and steamed
on the *HMS Herpes*
towards Argentina. I
like doggies on their "little
feet", don't you, I said, but
they kept rolling over, be-
neath the tracer bullets and
the Antarctic moon, beneath the
daunting missiles and the Prince
in his helicopter, they were
steaming towards interesting places,
to meet interesting people, and
kill them. They were at sea,
and it was also beneath them.

(Ted Berrigan &
Tom Pickard. Spring, '82)

Ted's Old Man

Ted's old man had trouble with the company
and, as a point of honour and self-respect,
died when they told him to go.

His old lady applied to a local party chief
who found her a job as a cashier
in the local school-meals cafeteria.

Ted said come round, Alice is interested
to talk and can remember folk's histories
a long way back: better than you could yourself.
It's scary, man, when they end up in poems.

Just shout up at the window
and I'll throw down the key.

My Radio, 1

its timing is perfect
and variable

its pronunciation
impeccable

its information
accurate

its sources
reliable

its correspondents
informed

its contents
incontestable

its motives
pure

it has many
voices

My Radio, 2

interprets the past
manages the present
and programs the future

my radio makes truth
sound false

my radio
is in complete control
and cannot be questioned

In Paradise

in paradise
I was ordered
to improvise

confident
of my co-operation
they paid in advance

it's the only sweatshop
in town

with a vacancy

My Pen

holds steady in my right hand:
black,
    with a silver top
and tight gold nib.

my **hero** pen
    made in the People's Republic of China,
and purchased in Warszawa
    by my wild, cloud-haired, Polish wife
with apple green eyes
    and twenty faces.

my **hero** pen
    joins vertical strokes
to curved and looping horizontals:
    sucks noisy and quick
when dipped in black India ink.

my **hero** pen
    speaks slim volumes,
running its incised beak
    along prescribed lines.

my **hero** pen
    feels good between
finger and thumb.

my **hero** pen
    purchased in Dom Ksiazki,
      on Nowy Swiat,
where walls of books
  are dripping ink
    and threaten to flood whole streets.

my ebony black,
    silver topped,
Golden Star, Seven 0 Five,
    Chinese,
hero pen
    looks good
  with a blue and chrome,
Three Seven One,
      YUEN CHANG—
made in Changhai,
    comma,
  China—
    best quality,
swivel-type stapler
    with four different uses.

my pen writes adverts
  for its comrades:

my pen shouldn't get
    too smart.

My pen's ink
    is the distilled dream
of fifty thousand million workers,
weary with clocking-in
  and clocking-out,
    signing-on
and signing-off:
  enslaved to machinery
of industry
    and state.

my pen refuses to recognize
   obsolete forms of government
and votes with its feet.

my pen wants to manage
   its own affairs,
thinking it knows best:

my pen demands
     complete autonomy.

Recipe: Pastime for the Unemployed

be mean with an onion
rip off its dried skin
and grip well

slice across its sphere
and chop

the onion will rise
into your nostrils
and speak to your eyes

keep slicing
weep and toss

into a hot iron pot
with chicken pieces

rib tickling each
with bay leaves

use what herbs there are to hand
allspice chilly
cloves and jogurt

decorate with saffron
sliced peel
from a fresh lemon

poke
with a fork

and don't let spitting fat
put you off

fight back

A Hole in Europe

One of two workers digging a hole
in a small square behind the old town's cathedral

is washing his muddy boots
with handfuls of water scooped from an icy pool.

A priest in black robes joins the diggers:
gazing down, as though granted a visa to Hell,
he hesitates, unable to afford the fare.

Led by a guide, a gang of tourists arrives,
wearing bright orange waterproof clothing.

This site, a monks medieval graveyard,
has been disturbed often.
The surrounding houses were built for rich merchants
during the Renaissance.

A charwife washes the steps of a nearby doorway
with a coloured cloth resembling the national flag.

The hole is due to the labourers
who worked all night sinking wooden shafts
to reach a burst water-pipe.

Pressing a thumb to his left nostril
he blows a snot two yards to the right.

As you can see it is raining heavily
and snowing intermittently.

The tourists drift towards the hole,
leaving the lecturer to guide alone.
Some take out sandwiches and alcohol.

Then all of them,
followed by the priest and guide,
descend the frail wooden ladder.

The charwife covers the hole with her rag,
placing a heavy stone on each flapping corner.

Going to a Friend's Trial

I was arrested and taken into an interview room
to meet the man I had indiscreetly slandered:
his name was Muscles.

I clutched a large blue notebook
in which my real crimes, and his, were listed.

You've been heard calling me a bastad, you little twat.
Fear staggered breath in my throat:
he had kicked several of my friends in the stomach.

Tweddle recklessly interrupted and demanded my release.
Howay Tommy.

Muscle's mate, Knucklenose, threw him out.

Am a bastad, eh?
One night soon we'll kick your door doon,
bop you one and bust you on a D and D.

Evidence
of my own illegitimacy
failed to placate him.

Cell Door: West-End Central

BB and DD were here
JAH LOVE
Horace snapt me stick
Budgie and Oggie Social Security fraud 83
kill spot checkers
Kings Cross Skins   Pat fitted-up
Jock the Fox   Body Beef   Animal
Jam Rider
Erika woz ere on warrant 83
Carol
from Cardiff
soliciting
PADDYS AND JOCKS
Taxi-door Lugs   Danny The Dancer   Tilbury Mods
Kevin=Jenny   Bounty Hunter
Gina I Love You Now and Forever by Lorraine Pollard
you deaf twats open the door
Izabel is having my baby I love her always
Mick Falls Road Belfast
Geordie from Jarrow near Newcastle-on-Tyne
MONEY TALKS
Anti Christ   Swansea Pete
Elaine Rogers 18.5.83 about ten past three I was
UP THE MINERS
Angel of Death
FUCK YOU
White Shadow
Jam Town Rockers   Diddy From Barnsley
LION
Raffael
PAPA   ZULU
Dave The Rave

Thirteen and a half hours without food—
worse than Russia

Chopin's Old Pianos

The Russians
    have thrown
from a third floor
    Warsaw window
Chopin
    's old piano,

said Vice President
  —finger on the button—
Bush.

But
    in many of his
client states
          composers
are thrown
        from windows,
their shredded hands
    flapping,
pulped by rifle butts
  in football stadiums.

As a sign—humanity
  and love
of the arts—
    tight security
has been mounted
    around
Chopin's old
  pianos:

hooked up
    to the roof
in lead-lined
   bunkers
they hang
    like carcasses
in a slaughter house.

Over dead composer cocktails
    and pin-ball holocaust
chess
    the banker generals
hear Chopin's
   music.

Stuffing wire cords
   into his mouth
they smash his teeth
with piano legs,
   punch fists full
of splintering ivory
   into his bleeding
      ears and
   anus.

Suspended
    by the tongue,
   Chopin
    is pulped
to a mush
    with his
   old pianos.

The music
   won't stop.

Skaman Report
Two letters from Lisa in Brixton

March 17, 1981

I'm living in Brixton now
in a squat on the infamous *frontline*,
it's got hot water plus electrics.
I'm trying to find a job,
which is virtually impossible,
and doing A levels at evening classes.

Most of my spare time is spent in pubs
and at gigs,
when we've got the money, which is rare
'cause the dole is only nineteen-fifty a week.

There's a huge rally for the unemployed
in Hyde Park next month—
with a load of good groups:
UB40; Specials; The Beat; Misty;
lots of Reggae and Ska.

In Brixton there's always a blues going on,
full of Rastas and spliffs. Great.

April 14, 1981

None of the papers have got any truth.
On Friday this bloke got stabbed
so some Rastas phones an ambulance.
While they were waiting the cops turned up
and grabbed the guy to question him.
They dumped him in the back of the squad car
and kept him, bleeding, for twenty minutes.
Eventually his friends dragged him away
to take him to the hospital
and the cops tries to do him (and a few others)
for resisting arrest.

On Saturday they had loads of cops on the beat
and five or six vans of SPG patrolling.
What provoked all the trouble
was really some undercover cops who,
after the police stopped a van and searched it,
started yelling and waving coshes.
The next thing was these blokes
pushed the policevan over and set it on fire.
I saw this just as I was turning the corner.
Then loads of cops with riot shields suddenly turned up
and tried to cordon off the area—
but crowds of blacks, gays, and punks
showered them with bricks and bottles.

Most of the reporters had their cameras smashed
but they let me take pictures.
One Rasta, who lives down the street, was saying
Take pictures of the opposition.
So I took one of six cops dragging
a fifteen year old kid up the street
and trying to bundle him into the van.
His mother was saying;
Let him walk!
but they wouldn't.
One cop whacked him round the face
so I said
Oy, don't do that! but another cop said:
We've got to have our fun.

Then everyone was saying
Let's burn down the George, which is
a totally prejudiced pub next door.
Crates of gin and beer were brought out
and passed around the crowd (black and white).
The Rasta was saying
Don't get drunk!
and another bloke started collecting all the bottles
into piles
and started making Molotov cocktails
with petrol
from one of the many cars
that were later burnt.
Then they looted up the road
and into Brixton
where most of the jewelry shops, Woolworths
and some clothes shops
got looted and burnt.

Sunday was mostly people from outside,
tourists who'd read in the paper
and came to look.
There were twenty vans
and ten coaches of police—
and helicopters flying about,
so nothing could really happen.
I saw loads of fire engines and cops
up by the prison.
At one point they cordoned off Railton Road
at both ends,
so some Rastas moved loads of instruments
and mikes into the street
and started jamming.
Soon a street party was going.
One bloke was telling the cops to join in
and saying
Black and white together, unite and fight together.
After about half an hour
the rioting started again.

I got a few cuts and bruises.

(Lisa Raworth and Tom Pickard)

Golden City Delivery Boy

1

a general's daughter
    prepares roast lamb
in an immaculate kitchen

polished mahogany tables
    stand dressed
wine decorked
    waiters grab an early bite

between the Tower
    and London Bridge
HMS Belfast
    meets the dreaming gaze
of an isolated banker
    on the twenty-ninth floor

the young Winston Churchill
    is coming to lunch

2

having delivered a selection
   of expensive delicacies
to the City Volunteer Club
   I joked
     to the pin-striped manager:

I've brought the pork pies

oh dear, another starf lunch,
   he replies

3

uniformed chauffeurs
    in shades
rabbit on Bentley bonnets

Rothschilds
    Bank of America
Bank of England
    Bankers Trust

Lonhro
    seagulls' eggs
Camembert
    Brie

Kuwait Investment Trust
  protected by
  bullet-proof glass walls
    which slide open
at a touch

Balls Brothers

the directors
    of the Bank of England
  take a daily delivery
    of Port Salut
  Sage Derby
    and dried fruit

when these gentlemen
  eat their prunes
and shit
  the pound will float
and we will swim in it

Spring Tide
For Basil Bunting,
Spring 1900 to Spring 1985

1

A filthy winter to have lived through,
dragged by the hair kicked and kicking into Spring

A year-long miner's strike,
broken.

Police road blocks blocked the motorways
and all roads leading to the north.

More reactionary than the thirties
the old fascist-fighting conchie told me.

2

While you lay dying in Hexham General Hospital,
we climbed Parliament Hill with our word-learner son
to see the city from the lip of the basin
and to see the kites.

The little Geordie-Polak cried *keats*
when he saw the rainbow-winged mosquitoes stringed
against the cockney clouds.

You wanted sleep, and a shot blood-clot
rushed to your brain. We pushed our faces into May:
snow-flower our blossom told us,
thanking frothing Hawthorn for the gift.

3

We stood by the North Sea:
a wash swirled around our feet.
Furthest from the shore
you stared towards a squall
on the dark horizon.

I warned against a threatening wave:
swelling,
it would overwhelm us.

Leaping to safety
I glanced back and saw you,
steady, silent, still,
measuring the trajectory
of the wave's engulfing curve.

My son's warm hand on my naked leg
woke me
drowning in a cold sweat.

You, the dark spring tide,
and the spring,
were gone.

Dawn Raid on an Orchard

Pebbles skipping off the window woke me.
Throwing off light blankets, night
became an unmade bed.
Shinning down a drainpipe skinned a knee.

Running soft in rubber shoes, trailing clouds of breath,
we knew that property was theft.

We wormed out where the wall was weakest
and found the broken glass on top was smashed.
Risking fingers and slashed feet we leapt.

The trees shook with blissful indignation
as we took ripe apples, tasting sweeter for the taking,
to fill our dads' redundant bait-bags.

A blackbird with a barbed-wire neck
cackled on a branch and clapped its wings. Flapping,
we dropped and lay flat as an alarm bell rang
in the gadgees gaff.

Franky sprained an ankle, and pain suppressed his laugh:
we howled silent, afraid of an alsation growling,
a police panda prowling past.

His mumpy jacket zipped-up and stuffed lumpy
with nocked-off fruit, he limped towards the orchard wall.
From the inside it looked much taller.
One day, we said, we'll mek it fall.